Avoiding the Ransom: Cybersecurity for Business Owners and Managers

Adam Levy

Adam Levy

For the last six years, Adam Levy has been the owner of Magnet Solutions Group (MagnetSolutionsGroup.com), an IT services and web development firm located in Austin, TX. Magnet Solutions Group works with businesses of all types in Central Texas and throughout the United States.

When he is not working, he enjoys playing hockey and exploring Texas with his wife Erika-- while trying as much great BBQ as they can.

Adam is also a frequent speaker on IT topics for business owners and managers.

Adam can be reached by email at Adam@MagnetSolutionsGroup.com.

Table of Contents

There are two types of companies: those that have been hacked and those that will be hacked.

Robert Mueller, FBI Director

Introduction

Recently, news was made when a close analysis of a photo of Mark Zuckerberg at Facebook headquarters revealed that he had placed a small piece of masking tape over the camera of his computer. People were surprised to find that the young tech CEO was almost certainly doing this as a security precaution against hackers taking illegal pictures or video of him. Though most business owners don't have a multi-million-dollar annual personal security budget and are not high-profile enough to attract attention from terrorist groups, the story is meaningful for small business owners as a wake-up call to the prevalence of business cybersecurity threats.

Even Facebook, a company employing some of the most talented network designers on earth, still knows that personnel practices can make a difference in defending a business.

Over the last several years, major cyberattacks and data breaches at prominent corporations and government agencies have attracted more and more media attention. The victims of these attacks include Anthem, the second largest healthcare provider in the US, the White House, the Pentagon, the US Government Office of Personnel Management, Sony Pictures, LinkedIn, DropBox, Target, Yahoo, eBay, JPMorgan Chase, Home Depot and Citibank. And of course a major undercurrent of the 2016 presidential election has been a series of hacks and data leaks, with the US accusing the Russian government of involvement.

However, despite all the deserved attention on these large, high profile attacks, today small businesses are actually being attacked by cybercriminals more frequently than large enterprises. Cybercriminals have moved down the food chain in a sense. Large enterprises are becoming more and more aware of the risks they face and investing in robust digital security and criminals recognize that the business and customer data that small and medium-sized businesses manage is increasingly valuable and that these businesses often lack comprehensive security defenses and effective personnel training.

For many small and medium-sized business owners across all industries, it requires a transition in thought to realize that one of their most valuable assets is the data they manage. This data—not the size of these businesses—makes them attractive targets to cybercriminals. As just one example of the value of this data, NPR reported that a single complete Medicare record of a patient can be sold on the black market for as much as $500. Furthermore, all businesses are becoming more and more interconnected as more activities and interactions take place digitally and more and more customer data is routinely collected. As more computers and digital devices enter the workplace, the 'attack surface' (in the parlance of cybersecurity) becomes bigger and more attractive. This broadening attack surface includes mobile devices and the 'internet of things,' with some estimates putting the number of connected devices that will be online in 2020 (both business and personal) at 200 billion (including perhaps 220 million connected cars). All of these newly connected devices that provide business productivity benefits also collect vast amounts of data that will need to be defended against exposure.

When a small business is attacked by cybercriminals, the effects can be devastating. Some experts suggest that the majority of small businesses that fall victim to a cyberattack are forced to close within a year. The software firm Kapersky Labs estimates that the total costs from an average cyberattack on a small business are $46,000.00. These costs can include expenses for attorney fees, IT consulting fees, network equipment replacement, lost productivity, and paying for credit monitoring services for customers. The effect on a company's reputation can be harder to quantify.

Of course, the government has been paying attention to these developments in the cyber threats to businesses and the regulations and liabilities of small businesses regarding their digital data have grown significantly over the last several years. So too has the enforcement activity by the government of these policies.

Despite all of this negative news about increased risks, there is good news on this front for business owners. The technology industry has recognized the need and the opportunity to devise solutions to protect businesses from these threats. A huge amount of resources has been dedicated to developing technologies that provide protection. And while the internet has certainly provided one of the avenues of attack for criminals, it has also provided the means for economical, remote monitoring and defense solutions that can offer constant vigilance, reduced liability and peace-of-mind for business owners.

The purpose of this book is to outline the nature of the threats facing small and medium-sized businesses today as well as the basic steps that should be taken to minimize the risks of an attack and to mitigate the effects of any attack that does take place. Fortunately, these effective cybersecurity practices need not be hugely expensive or extremely difficult to adopt.

In fact, as you'll see throughout the book, the major steps to take are fairly straightforward. They include things like having appropriate and updated security software, well-designed networks and firewalls, on-going remote monitoring, cloud-based data back-up and smart employee technology practices. Technology is empowering small businesses today to do amazing things. This technology also presents risks, but those risks can be managed effectively. The smart practice is to be pro-active and understand that digital security is now a part of doing business.

Crime has always been a regrettably consistent element of the human experience.

MARK FROST, *The List of Seven*

Chapter 1. A Brief History of Cybercrime

In 2016, cybercrime is a well-recognized term for illicit activities taking place in the digital realm. 'Cyberattacks', 'hacking', 'phishing' 'malware' and similar terms are part of the popular vernacular. But this familiarity with digital crime is a recent development. The term 'virus' was only first used in relation to computer software in 1983. So how did computer and internet crimes evolve? Here's a brief history highlighting some of the major developments and incidents in a criminal history that is both scary and fascinating.

Rene Carmille

One of the earliest examples of computer 'crime' happens to also be one of the most inspiring. Rene Carmille was the comptroller general of the French Army and a leading technocrat in France during World War II. He kept the French military tabulators (punch card-based information processing machines that were pre-cursors to modern computers) from the Nazi regime and created Vichy France's Demographic Service, which was tasked by the Nazis with providing them with census data. These census data were to also include lists of Jews, who were to be rounded up and sent to death camps.

Specifically, Carmille's office was responsible for making sure that census data was transferred onto the punch cards. While ostensibly working in collaboration with the Nazi regime, Carmille was in fact using the information to help organize the French Resistance and undermine the Nazis' campaign of murdering Jews. Column 11 of each punch card designated a person's religion—Carmille's office never punched any designation in column 11. Carmille was eventually discovered and captured by the Nazis. Under torture, he revealed no information. Carmille was sent to Dachau, where he was killed.

The Tech Model Railroad Club

In the 1960s, students at MIT who were members of the Tech Model Railroad Club (TMRC) used the term 'hacker' to refer to themselves and their work in 'hacking' more elegant solutions to the electronic systems used in these toy trains. They were some of the first computer hackers as well, working on the mainframes at MIT.

John Draper and Phreaking

In 1971, an Esquire magazine article featured a Las Vegas resident named John Draper, a retired Air Force technician, who had developed a 'blue box' that allowed for free telephone calls to be made over AT&T's network. Draper is one of the earliest and most well-known hackers. Draper had learned that a toy whistle that was being given away as a child's toy in Cap'n Crunch cereal at the time could be used to create a tone at exactly 2600 hertz—and that that frequency could be used to exploit a vulnerability in call-routing switches that used in-band signaling, allowing for free calls to be placed. Based on this information, Draper devised a 'blue box'—an electronic device that produced other sound frequencies used by AT&T. It essentially allowed its users to act as illicit telephone operators and place free calls. Draper and other 'phreakers' were hacking the newly all-electronic phone network switching system. Draper was subsequently arrested, convicted of toll fraud and sentenced to five years of probation.

Draper's influence in the hacking and computer worlds is still felt today. He was an acquaintance of Apple co-founders Steve Wozniack and Steve Jobs and was a member with them in the legendary Homebrew Computer Club of Silicon Valley, which was instrumental in the launching of the personal computer revolution. (Notice that the Homebrew Computer Club focused on personal computers now, after the Tech Model Railroad Club had focused on mainframes.) And the name of the quarterly hacking publication is still *2600*, a reference to the frequency used by the blue boxes. Many hackers also still use the handle 'Cap'n Crunch.'

Gary Thuerk and the First Spam

In 1978 the first spam email was sent out to recipients who didn't ask for it, starting a pattern that has been repeated billions and billions of times in the years since. Ironically enough, the first spam email was an advertising email for a new computer, sent by Gary Thuerk, a marketing executive at Digital Equipment Corporation. Gary sent it out over ARPAnet, the Defense Department network that preceded the internet. He apparently thought there would be some interest in the computer he was advertising, but also anticipated some negative feedback (correctly, as it turned out).

Elk Cloner

One of the earliest and most well-known computer viruses was developed by 15 year-old high school student Rich Skrenta in 1982. Called Elk Cloner, it actually targeted Apple II computers, and preceded viruses targeting PCs. The virus was hidden on a floppy disk that loaded it onto the computer. After every 50 boot-up attempts, a poem would come on the screen:

Elk Cloner: The program with a personality

It will get on all your disks
It will infiltrate your chips
Yes, it's Cloner!

It will stick to you like glue
It will modify RAM too
Send in the Cloner!

Rich's 'cloner' program was not called a virus at the time, as the term 'virus' in reference to malicious, self-replicating software programs would not be coined until 1983.

The 414s and Los Alamos

One of the earliest and most famous incidents of hacking was a remarkable case of life imitating art. In the summer of 1983, the hit movie WarGames came out. WarGames starred Matthew Broderick as a nice, middle class teenager who almost starts World War III by hacking into the Department of Defense from his bedroom and accessing the US nuclear arsenal.

On the same day of the release of WarGames, June 3, 1983, the Sloan Kettering Cancer Center was hacked into (it was not a hard target: both the username *and* the password to the network were 'test') and $1,500.00 worth of medical bills were deleted in an attempt by the hackers to cover their trail. An administrator noticed the deleted bills and contacted the FBI. The FBI realized that the hackers had played computer games installed inside the network and so set a trap by installing another game they hoped the hackers would play on a return visit. The scheme worked and the hackers were traced via phone records on their next visit.

The FBI had discovered the 414s (ages 16-22). They were a group of hackers working off of their home computers in their bedrooms who had hacked into prominent computer systems, including the Los Alamos National Laboratory. Their goals weren't malicious—they liked to play video games located inside these business networks.

The 414s became a media sensation. All but two of the members were not charged, as they were minors. The two that were prosecuted faced charges of 'making harrassing telephone calls,' as there were no statutes against hacking or computer crimes on the books at that time. One of the 414s, 17 year-old Neil Patrick, became a short-lived celebrity, appearing the cover of Newsweek and testifying in front of Congress as it introduced new bills to tackle cybercrime.

The Morris Worm

In 1988 Robert Morris was a graduate student at Cornell when he launched the 'Morris Worm,' which is considered to be the first worm on the internet. Worms are self-replicating pieces of malicious software. The Morris Worm spread to thousands of computers and resulted in tens of millions of dollars of damages. Morris became the first person convicted under the 1986 Computer Fraud and Abuse Act. Morris claimed he was trying to highlight the vulnerabilities in the emerging internet—which he certainly did. After being sentenced to three years probation, Robert subsequently sold an ecommerce platform to Yahoo for millions of dollars, started the successful tech funding firm Y Combinator and ended up as a tenured professor of electrical engineering and computer science at MIT.

The 'AIDS' Trojan

A year later, the first and most famous 'trojan horse' software attack took place—and laid the conceptual basis for modern ransomware extortion. Trojan horse software is malicious code that gets downloaded onto a computer when installing seemingly benign software. In

1989 20,000 floppy disks stamped 'PC Cyborg Corporation' arrived on the desks of AIDS researchers in more than 90 countries. The disks claimed to have an AIDS education software—they did, in fact, have a program that measured a person's risk of contracting AIDS based on their responses to a survey. But the disks also contained the 'AIDS' Trojan, a virus that ultimately encrypted the victims' files. Dramatically, users were instructed to turn on their printers and a printed ransom note demanded payment of $189 be sent to a Panamanian PO Box in exchange for a decryption key. Though the 'AIDS' Trojan did cause much damage—many institutions deleted valuable data in response—the encryption used was ultimately decipherable and decryption keys were distributed to victims. The perpetrator turned out to be an evolutionary biologist from England named Joseph L. Popp. Some speculated that his motivation arose from having been denied a job at the WHO—many of his victims had been attendees at the WHO International AIDS Conference. However, he was determined to be mentally unstable and unfit to stand trial and never received any punishment for his brazen cybercrime.

AOHell

In 1997, a software program by the name of AOHell was released by the hackers known as Da Chronic and J-Why. Users of AOL in the 1990s had already coined the term 'AOHell' to refer to the experience of dealing with slow connection speeds and other issues in using AOL. The AOHell software played on that term, but actually created an experience that was closer to hell. The software manipulated the interface of AOL and generally created havoc, allowing users to create fake user accounts, steal user AOL passwords and credit card numbers, automatically sign-off other users from AOL, send automated emails to fill up users' inboxes and flood chat rooms with offensive art.

AOHell was notable for contributing precedents for two future trends in cybercrime. The first trend was phishing. AOHell contained what it called a 'fisher' tool to steal information. It would send an instant message to other users claiming to be AOL Customer Service and asking them to confirm sensitive data. The second precedent set was that of 'crimeware': malicious software that could be copied, bought and sold, and used by hackers with limited technical skills. AOHell's code was copied into hundreds of similar programs and used by many hackers who did not possess the skills to devise such programs themselves.

Denial of Service Attacks

In February 2000, one of the earliest and largest Denial-of-Service (DoS) attacks took down prominent websites including eBay, CNN, E-Trade, Yahoo! and Amazon.   Denial-of-Service attacks involve either crashing websites or reducing their response to a crawl by flooding a network with more packets of data or information requests than it can handle. These attacks gained so much notoriety that they prompted President Bill Clinton to convene an emergency cyber-security summit in which Attorney General Janet Reno promised that the Justice Department would not rest until the perpetrator was arrested.

The culprit behind these attacks? Michael Calce (better known by his hacker name, Mafiaboy), a 15 year-old Canadian hacker working from his home computer, who was ultimately arrested while watching Goodfellas at a sleepover at a friend's house. Denial-of-Service and Distributed Denial-of-Service (DDoS) attacks (launched simultaneously from multiple IP addresses) initially started out as pranks by hackers looking for a rush or to show-off their skills, but are now used to threaten and extort money from website owners.

Botnets

Today, it's estimated that millions of computers world-wide are under the control of cybercriminals. These computers—called zombies—are usually brought under control through Trojan software that users have downloaded unknowingly. Most often, these computer owners do not know that their computer's processing power can be called upon by hackers when they want to. These zombie computers are organized into networks called Botnets, which can be called upon to deliver spam, phishing attempts or DDoS attacks. The first mass attempt to create a Botnet is thought to be the SoBig email worm of 2003.

Stuxnet

Stuxnet was a computer worm that targeted computers involved in the Iranian government's uranium enrichment program in 2010. The worm attacked vulnerabilities in Windows and then undermined the software that interfaces with and controls actual physical, mechanical processes in the plants. Stuxnet caused a good number of Iranian centrifuges to spin out of control and destroy themselves, all the while having the software that monitors the mechanical activity in the plant report that everything looked normal. Though nobody has officially taken responsibility for Stuxnet, it is widely believed that it was developed as a joint effort of the United States and Israel to undermine the Iranian nuclear arms efforts in a way that made it look to the Iranians as though they had simply suffered technical errors. Stuxnet is significant for a couple of reasons. If the US and Israeli governments were behind it, it represents one of the first documented efforts to destroy physical architecture through a cyberattack. It also serves as a possible foreshadowing of cyberattacks on businesses in the future, where connected mechanical business processes are targeted.

It is the mark of a truly intelligent person to be moved by statistics.

George Bernard Shaw

Chapter 2. Today's Threat Landscape

In today's business environment, cyber-attacks are, unfortunately, a part of doing business that has to be addressed.   While most of the attention is typically directed at the highest profile attacks on government agencies, large corporations and political and entertainment figures, the fact remains that small and medium-sized businesses are the most frequent targets of cyberattacks.

In fact, the threat to small business from cybercriminals has reached a point where it has begun to attract Congressional attention.   In 2016, House of Representatives Small Business

Committee Chairman Steve Chabot declared that "The owners, employees and customers of America's 28 million small businesses need to have confidence that their data is secure."

Let's take a look at some of the statistics, which are sobering.

- A 2016 study by the Ponemon Institute found that more than 50% of small businesses have had their computers breached in the last 12 months.

- The same study by the Ponemon Institute found that only 14% of the small businesses surveyed rated their ability to mitigate cyber- attacks as highly effective, 59% claimed to have no knowledge of their employees' password practices and 65% do not enforce their existing password policies.

- A 2015 survey of 500 small businesses by the insurer Nationwide found that 8 in 10 small businesses don't have a cyberattack response plan.

- Cybersecurity software firm Symantec discovered more than 430 million new pieces of malware in 2015, a 36% rise from 2014.

- Also according to Symantec, over half a billion personal information records were lost or stolen in 2015.

- Malware attacks on Linux and Mac operating systems rose significantly in 2015.

- In 2015, there was more than one new zero-day vulnerability discovered each week.

- 16% of malware is now able to exploit virtualized machines according to Symantec.

- According to the FBI, ransomware-related ransom payments in the US totaled $24 million in all of 2015 and jumped to $200 million in just the first quarter of 2016.

- Research by Towergate Insurance revealed that 82% of small business owners believe they are not targets for attacks because they don't feel they have any data worth stealing.

- According to Symantec, in 2015 43% of sophisticated, resource-intensive targeted spear-phishing attacks were actually directed at small businesses, compared with 34% in 2014.

Why Are Small and Medium-Sized Businesses Attractive Targets?

There are a couple of major reasons that small and mid-sized businesses are facing increased attention from cybercriminals today. The first reason is that small businesses increasingly store more and more valuable digital data as more and more business is handled by computers and digital devices. Though these businesses may not focus on this or even be aware of the extent to which they're accumulating this data, regular business practices collect valuable data about businesses practices (costs, pricing, intellectual property, employee records) and customers (credit card numbers, passwords, names, family relationships, demographic information and in some cases financial and medical records).

The second major reason in that small and medium-sized businesses generally have less robust cyber defenses in place than enterprises. This makes these targets 'softer' than larger corporations or government agencies, but still significantly more valuable than individual consumers.

The final major reason is that small and medium-sized businesses are a very large pool of targets—the vast majority of all businesses. And as cybercrime has become commoditized and automated—allowing for cheap, widespread attacks on many businesses simultaneously—the ability to ensure that at least some attacks on such a large set of potential victims will be successful has increased.

The example of zero day vulnerabilities and their exploitation is a good example of this rapid, systematized and inexpensive attack protocol. A vulnerability in a widely distributed piece of software will be discovered and added quickly to the toolkits that cybercriminals use. Very soon after, attacks will be directed at millions of potentially vulnerable computers and many of those that have not been patched in time will be exploited successfully.

Who Are the Cybercriminals?

In cybersecurity parlance, cybercriminals are widely referred to as 'threat actors.' So who are the threat actors out there today that are targeting businesses?

The first group of criminals—and perhaps the largest—are simply amateur hackers. Though using the name amateur may make them sound less threatening, these amateur hackers have access to tools and software that can be purchased that allow them to be very effective with a very limited amount of technical knowledge.

The second group is professional hackers. Many of these criminals today act professionally and are highly organized into criminal enterprises. These actors can launch sophisticated attacks. In fact, many of these hackers have their own areas of specialization.

So-called 'hacktivist' communities are groups of hackers that perform attacks motivated by political or social grievances. Hacktivists tend not to be a regular threat to small and medium-sized businesses.

Terrorist groups have also become involved in hacking and illegal attacks in the digital world, but do not currently pose a significant threat to small and mid-sized businesses.

Nation states have increasingly become involved in digital hacking. However, it is important to note that these actors usually target other governments or major corporations, though a small business with valuable intellectual property might present an attractive target to some nation states that engage in digital commercial espionage.

Finally, it's important to note that company insiders can pose a threat as well. Many businesses face digital attacks—be it theft or vandalism—from unhappy employees or former employees that have retained access to their network credentials.

What Are The Types of Attacks?

There are several different types of cyberattacks that are common today. Malware is the most common threat affecting small and mid-sized businesses. 99% of current malware attacks are initiated through phishing emails.

Social Engineering

Social engineering attacks are designed to exploit human trust to gain access to computer or network credentials. Phishing emails are an example of social engineering when they trick employees into giving away passwords or other information. Another form of social engineering that has emerged is stealing credentials to executives at a business and then posing as that executive in emails to subordinates. Cybercriminals have successfully used such strategies to have employees make seemingly legitimate business payments to criminal accounts.

One other form of social engineering that is worth noting is fake 'technical support' attacks. Though these attacks typically have focused on consumers, they have been successfully used against businesses as well. In these attacks, a criminal poses as technical support from a technology company like Microsoft in an email or phone call and gains access to a network by asking the victim for computer credentials to resolve a non-existent technical issue.

Hacking

Hacking attacks are when cybercriminals work to access a business network. Hackers usually target un-patched known vulnerabilities. A subset of these types of attacks are advanced persistent threats (APTs), which are long-term targeted attacks that break into a network and often seek to remain hidden within the network for extended durations. APTs are less commonly directed at smaller businesses and more frequently target enterprises.

Denial-of-Service Attacks

Denial-of-Service (DoS) attacks target servers from either a single or multiple IP addresses simultaneously with the goals of overloading those servers with information requests, causing the servers to stop working or to be unable to process requests from legitimate users. DoS attacks are used to bring down networks and company websites.

Malvertising

Malvertising is online digital advertising—often placed on legitimate websites—that when clicked upon can download malware into a computer and network. The instances of malvertising have increased significantly over the last several years. Research by software maker

Cyphort indicates that the rates of infected ads online have increased 325% from 2014 to 2015.

Human Error

Finally, it's worth noting that human error is one of the most significant causes of network breaches and data loss for small and medium-sized businesses. An employee might simply lose unprotected mobile device and end up leaving valuable data or network access out in the open for any criminal to take. It is not an infrequent occurrence.

Ransomware is more about manipulating vulnerabilities in human psychology than the adversary's technological sophistication.

James Scott, Sr. Fellow, Institute for Critical Infrastructure Technology

Chapter 3. Ransomware

2 4 million dollars was the total amount paid in the United States in 2015 in ransoms related to ransomware, as estimated by the FBI. That amount represents the total for the entire year. In just the first quarter of 2016, the FBI reports that ransom payments related to ransomware in the US totaled $200 million. Some in the industry are estimating that the total will reach $1 billion for all of 2016. Ransomware attacks have entered the popular consciousness and they have become the most common—and costly—cyber threat facing small and medium-sized businesses today. So what is ransomware exactly, why is it so popular a tool for cybercriminals and how can you protect your business from it?

What Is Ransomware?

Ransomware sounds scary--and it is actually scary. It's a type of malware that holds your data (and sometimes your network and even identity) hostage by encrypting it until you pay the author of the malware to 'release' your data by providing a decryption key. There's often a threat that your data will be destroyed in periodic installments if you don't pay. So, like kidnappings for ransom in the real world, the motivation is to make money.

Ransomware in various forms has been around since the 1980s, but it really came to the public's attention starting in September 2013 when the ransomware CryptoLocker began holding Windows computers in the US hostage using Bitcoin digital currency to collect the ransom payments. CryptoLocker was eventually solved by an international police operation, but successors, like CryptoWall, have taken its place. CryptoWall has driven an estimated 325 million dollars in ransom payments.

Ransomware is the most prevalent cybersecurity threat facing businesses in all industries today. According the to the cybersecurity software firm Symantec, in 2015 alone, 362,000 new variants of ransomware were identified.

How Does A Ransomware Attack Happen?

Ransomware usually accesses a computer or network through predictable avenues: phishing emails, unpatched software programs, software downloads, malicious websites or 'malvertisements'—infected advertisements that on legitimate websites that can be infectious when clicked on.

In the context of ransomware, phishing emails are attempts by cybercriminals to get employees to download ransomware onto their computer and network. 99% of all ransomware attacks are initiated through email.

Phishing emails can usually be identified by some characteristic features. Phishing emails often contain links directly in the email message. In particular, they can often have links that lead directly to '.exe' files. Phishing emails will often try to appear as though they're coming from a major company. Often a major tech company, like Google, Microsoft or Facebook. They may even be associated with fake websites that look similar to the major company's website. These emails also often contain threats or urgent calls to action, suggesting there's been irregular activity in your account and it will be closed if you don't act *now*.

Whether coming from a phishing email or some other source, once the ransomware has infected a computer it will begin encrypting the files on that computer. The most common form of encryption used in webmail is RSA 2048, which is effectively impenetrable without a decryption key. Ransomware will not just encrypt files on the computer it was downloaded onto; it will spread across the network and encrypt files throughout the business. The net effect is that one accidental download of ransomware by a team member can quickly encrypt all of the files across a network.

Once at least some the files are encrypted, the cybercriminals will display a screen on the affected computer or a link to a website notifying you that you've been attacked. Unlike some other types of hacking attacks, ransomware only profits the criminals when the victim is aware that they've been attacked. This page will have the 'ransom note.' It will usually include a deadline for making a payment (usually through the e-currency Bitcoin), along with instructions for making the payment. It will also often have a threat that the encrypted data will be destroyed if the ransom payment is not made. If the ransom is paid, the hackers promise to provide decryption software.

How to Respond to An Attack

If you are attacked, it is possible that the ransomware being used is a recognizable variant and there may be the possibility of decrypting your data. Outside of this scenario, if there is no data back-up to access, the only option becomes paying the ransom to retrieve the data—a route followed by many victims.

It's worth noting that the FBI recommends not paying ransomware ransoms, both for moral reasons and because it does not guarantee that access to the encrypted data will be given. James Trainor, FBI Cyber Division Assistant Director, has offered this reasoning on not paying ransoms:

> "Paying a ransom doesn't guarantee an organization that it will get its data back— we've seen cases where organizations never got a decryption key after having paid the ransom. Paying a ransom not only emboldens current cyber criminals to target more organizations, it also offers an incentive for other criminals to get involved in this type of illegal activity. And finally, by paying a ransom, an organization might inadvertently be funding other illicit activity associated with criminals."

Security Measures

Many businesses become attentive to preventative measures after they've been attacked. Don't wait for that to happen. There are definite steps your business can start taking today to not only lessen the chances of falling victim to a ransomware attack, but also decreasing the negative impact of an attack.

The single most important step that you can take is to have an effective, regularly tested data back-up and business continuity solution in place. If your business data is being backed up regularly and securely and that data can be retrieved and accessed quickly, ransomware does not pose a threat to you. Even if your data on your network is encrypted, you can retrieve your back-ups of that data from their remote location.

Make sure that you have up-to-date anti-malware and anti-virus solutions installed on all of the endpoints in your network. Also make sure that security patches are installed and up-to-date for your software. (These are regular maintenance services that an IT services firm will usually provide as part of a managed services solution.) Intelligently limiting user access to only needed areas of the network can also play a role in limiting the files that are encrypted should a ransomware attack happen.

It's also critical that everybody at the practice knows how to identify phishing emails and is reminded regularly to be wary of unsolicited email. Nobody should ever click on a link in an unsolicited email—there's no reason to do it. If you do receive an unsolicited email and you're unsure if it's legitimate and from a business that you deal with, simply call up that business that appears to be sending the email.

Furthermore, employees should be aware of phone calls purportedly from technology companies like Microsoft or others asking for computer passwords and credentials to be able to take care of supposed technology support issues. Exploiting natural human tendencies toward trust and routine is a key piece of successful ransomware attacks.

The ransomware threat continues to grow, unfortunately. On the black market today, there are even ransomware-as-a-service subscriptions available, making it even easier for non-technical criminals to leverage these types of attacks. At a very minimum, every business today should have a cloud-based, actively managed data back-up system in place.

Those who cannot remember the past are condemned to repeat it.

George Santayana

Chapter 4. Case Studies 1: Police Departments

For those business owners and managers that think 'this could never happen to us' the following cases ought to give you pause. Police departments around the country have been targeted—successfully—by cybercriminals and the outcomes of the attacks have led many departments to make the decision to pay a ransom to retrieve their data, even though they have extensive law enforcement resources to call upon and even though it goes against their own ethos of not paying ransoms and against the official advice of the FBI.

Many police stations in the US have been attacked by ransomware in the last couple of years and the trend seems to be increasing. Last year, the Tewksbury, MA police department was faced with a CryptoLocker attack. The attack came to the department's attention with what seemed like typical network difficulty;

personnel had trouble pulling up arrest records. Then a message appeared on a computer screen:

"Your personal files are encrypted. File decryption costs ~ $500. If you really value your data, then we suggest you do not waste valuable time searching for other solutions because they do not exist."

The department's back-up was an external hard-drive that was also infected (their most recent un-infected back-up was over 18 months old). Federal and state experts (including the Department of Homeland Security and the Massachusetts State Police) along with private security firms spent five days trying to decrypt the files—unsuccessfully. The Tewksbury Police Department ultimately paid about $500 in Bitcoin to retrieve their data. The Tewksbury Police Chief Timothy Sheehan was quoted in the Tewksbury Town Crier:

"It was an eye-opening experience, I can tell you right now. It made you feel that you lost control of everything. Paying the Bitcoin ransom was the last resort."

The attack in Tewksbury was not unique. The Swansea, MA Police Department was also hit with a ransomware attack in 2013 and ultimately paid about $750.00 in Bitcoin to retrieve its data. In January of 2015 the Midlothian, IL Police Department paid a $500 ransom to anonymous cybercriminals after a

Cryptoware attack that also encrypted its back-up files. There have been several more reported attacks and many in the police community feel that there have almost certainly been many more attacks that have gone unreported.

In 2014, a malware attack in Durham, NH started when an employee clicked on a link in an email attachment apparently coming from somebody the department knew. (It looked like a digital fax attached to an email about an ongoing investigation.) All of the department's files were encrypted by the next morning. However, the Durham department chose not to pay a ransom because they had a full, recent back-up of all their files.   They did have to clean their computers and re-load their data, but they were not at the mercy of the cybercriminals.

Also in 2014, the Collinsville, AL police department was attacked by ransomware, which was inadvertently downloaded from an email attachment. Seven computers were infected, including those that housed files containing police video and mugshots. Even after assistance from the FBI, the files could not be decrypted. Police Chief Gary Bowen refused to pay the ransom and the files were never recovered.

In April of 2015, the Lincoln County, Maine Sherrif's Office fell victim to a ransomware attack when a recently unused computer that had been infected was plugged back into the network. Their data back-up could not help them because they had an error in their back-up procedure that they had been unaware of. Sheriff Todd Brackett and his advisors decided to pay the ransom of about $300 and they received their decryption key. Sheriff Brackett then decided to cancel the Bitcoin ransom payment after receiving the key. Two days later they were forced to pay about $500 for a new decryption key after a second attack. The FBI tracked the payment to Switzerland but then lost the trail.

Police departments are attractive targets for cybercriminals for some of the same key reasons that small businesses are attractive targets. According to the Bureau of Justice Statistics, about half of all police departments in the US have fewer than 10 officers and don't have extensive in-house IT capabilities. Data security and back-up have not traditionally been priorities. They're also attractive to cybercriminals employing ransomware because they are known to have critical operations that can't go down for significant periods. Cybercriminals know that many departments will make a simple cost-benefit analysis and choose to pay a small ransom to retrieve their data. And with automation and ease of sending out thousands of ransomware-infected emails simultaneously, the profits to be had from collecting may small ransoms are significant.

The FBI officially advises against paying ransoms. But in practice, the need to pay ransoms is a reality that its agents have acknowledged. At the 2015 Cyber Security Summit, Joseph Bonavolonta, Assistant Special Agent in Charge of the FBI's CYBER and Counterintelligence Program made news when he said

"The ransomware is that good. To be honest, we often advise people just to pay the ransom."

The FBI later followed up by telling the computer security news site Naked Security:

"The FBI doesn't make recommendations to companies; instead, the Bureau explains what the options are for businesses that are affected and how it's up to individual companies to decide for themselves the best way to proceed. That is, either revert to back up systems, contact a security professional, or pay."

Better be despised for too anxious apprehensions,
than ruined by too confident security.

Edmund Burke

Chapter 5. Case Studies 2: LabMD

The case of LabMD is a cautionary tale for any small business about the potential hazards of data leaks and insufficient security protocols today. It's also a landmark case that is now being appealed in the federal courts by high-profile data security litigators. Finally, it also happens to be a long and fascinating tale about small business, political influence and US government regulation practices that has actually led to a book, "The Devil Inside the Belway."

In 2008, Michael Daugherty was a small business owner in Atlanta. His company, LabMD, tested blood and specimens for urologists and had nearly $5 million in annual sales. That spring he received a call from a company called Tiversa that claimed that they had found a LabMD document online that contained the protected health information of thousands of patients. This would be a major violation of HIPAA rules.

LabMD quickly identified the source of the leak: their billing manager had downloaded the consumer file sharing app Limewire, in violation of company policy, and had accidentally left the file with patient data available for sharing. LabMD quickly removed Limewire from their computer and spent months scouring the internet to determine whether the files had been downloaded or shared elsewhere on the internet. They could find no evidence that this had happened. It appeared that only Tiversa had actually downloaded the file.

Tiversa was a company that used software to monitor peer-to-peer networks for its clients to see what they were sharing. Tiversa offered—at a cost of $475.00 per hour, amounting to tens of thousands of dollars—to determine the source of the leak and contain it. Tiversa talked about the reputational damage that such a leak could cause LabMD. Daugherty felt that Tiversa was essentially trying to extort him and declined to engage their services. Tiversa then claimed they were worried about their own liability if they didn't report this 'breach' to the FTC.

In 2010, the FTC Division of Privacy and Identity Protection notified LabMD that they were investigating it due to their discovery of a file with patient data being available on a peer-to-peer network. The FTC required LabMD to answer myriad questions about its technology use—down to the use of individual routers and firewalls—and any documentation of exposure of protected patient information.

You might be wondering why the FTC is the agency that started investigating. The FTC has a history of overseeing digital data issues, even though its authority to do so is disputed. The Federal Trade Commission Act prohibits "unfair or deceptive acts or practices in or affecting commerce." Since 2000, the FTC has interpreted this language as allowing it to govern commercial data security. The idea here is that if a business doesn't sufficiently protect its customers' data, it's engaging in unfair or deceptive acts. Prior to LabMD, every company that the FTC brought a digital data case against settled. The companies don't admit wrongdoing, and they often agree to years of security audits by outside firms.

LabMD chose not to settle. Michael Daugherty felt that a settlement—which the FTC would announce in a press release—would undermine the confidence of LabMD's customers and ruin his business. He also felt the FTC was being unreasonable, as LabMD had immediately remedied the breach, had been cooperative with the FTC investigation and had invested hundreds of thousands of dollars in upgrading its IT system to address security shortcomings.

The FTC investigation was onerous. (Daugherty actually felt that it was punitive and designed to force companies to settle, rather than deal with the strain of an investigation.)

Some of the details of the investigation are indeed eyebrow-raising. When LabMD initially mailed thousands of pages of documents to the FTC offices in Washington, DC, the agency demanded that they be re-sent by FedEx. Later, the agency demanded over 20 depositions—including some from people no longer employed by the company—be delivered on the same day at locations around the country. LabMD was forced to hire a Washington-based law firm experienced in such issues to represent it.

One of the issues involved that angered Daugherty was that Tiversa did not seem like a legitimate company. They had essentially breached LabMD's data and that ill-gotten information was basically serving as the FTC's basis for its case against LabMD. The only person who seemed to listen to this argument was the FTC Commissioner at the time, J. Thomas Rosch. Rosch stated in a dissent in 2012 that Tiversa "is a commercial entity that has a financial interest in intentionally exposing and capturing sensitive files on computer networks, and a business model of offering its services to help organizations protect against similar infiltrations." Rosch argued the FTC shouldn't use such information, but he was overruled.

In fact, a former employee of Tiversa would later tell Daugherty that Tiversa had not found any of the patient files downloaded anywhere else on the internet and that Tiversa had notified the FTC out of spite when LabMD refused to use their services. This employee claimed that Tiversa had intentionally submitted a false list of places on the internet to the FTC where the files had supposedly been downloaded. The House Oversight Committee would eventually start investigating Tiversa. That investigation would eventually reveal that Tiversa had faked evidence of data leaks to win clients and had a long-standing relationship with the FTC, providing the names of many companies the agency would subsequently investigate. The FBI would later raid Tiversa's offices in Pittsburgh during an investigation of whether it provided false information to the FTC. (Daugherty has filed suit against Tiversa for hacking LabMD's computers.)

Another issue was that the FTC doesn't publish guidelines for businesses about what constitutes satisfactory data security standards. The only source of information for businesses are the consent decrees published by the FTC in press releases about companies that had settled. These decrees amount to a sort of 'common law' about data security practices.

In 2013 the FTC filed a formal complaint against LabMD. LabMD had spent over $500,000.00 on legal fees by this point and their annual revenue had declined by nearly half. Employees blamed Daugherty for not settling. LabMD's insurance companies were unwilling to renew its policies. In 2014, the company closed after 18 years in business.

The case initially was tried in the FTC's administrative court system. In a surprise, the Administrative Law Judge hearing that case ruled strongly in favor of LabMD, claiming that the evidence against it, provided by Tiversa, was not trustworthy and that the FTC did not meet its burden of proof. However, the FTC appealed that ruling to the full commission of the FTC, which ruled against LabMD this summer. The FTC argued that, even without the false Tiversa claims of data downloads of patient information, the exposure of the data in and of itself constituted unfair and deceptive trade practices.

The FTC published this summary of the case following the ruling against LabMD:

'The Federal Trade Commission filed a complaint against medical testing laboratory LabMD, Inc. alleging that the company failed to reasonably protect the security of consumers' personal data, including medical information. The complaint alleges that in two separate incidents, LabMD collectively exposed the personal information of approximately 10,000 consumers. The complaint alleges that LabMD billing information for over 9,000 consumers was found on a peer-to-peer (P2P) file-sharing network and then, in 2012, LabMD documents containing sensitive personal information of at least 500 consumers were found in the hands of identity thieves. The case is part of an ongoing effort by the Commission to ensure that companies take reasonable and appropriate measures to protect consumers' personal data.'

In the unanimous decision against LabMD, FTC Chairwoman Edith Ramirez claimed that "LabMD's security practices were unreasonable, lacking even basic precautions to protect the sensitive consumer information maintained on its computer system. Among other things, it failed to use an intrusion detection system or file integrity monitoring; neglected to monitor traffic coming across its firewalls; provided essentially no data security training to its employees; and never deleted any of the consumer data it had collected."

Michael Daugherty has said that he was hoping for such a ruling against LabMD by the FTC so that he can appeal the case in federal court. Following the ruling, he issued a statement saying that "The FTC has spent untold taxpayer dollars investigating LabMD, destroying jobs and usurping power over patient information from the U.S. Department of Health and Human Services." The hotel chain Wyndham is also challenging the FTC's authority to regulate data security standards and major trade groups like the Chamber of Commerce, TechFreedom, the National Federation of Independent Businesses and the International Franchise Association have filed motions supporting Wyndham and LabMD.

The Implications For Business Cybersecurity

The federal LabMD case is important for several reasons and will be watched closely by the cybersecurity and IT community. It will most likely define the FTC's role as the chief regulator of business cybersecurity practices. The FTC seems to be expanding its authority to regulate cybersecurity—authority that is not explicitly listed in the law. It also appears to be arguing that it can sanction businesses merely for having a security breach, even if no actual harm or injury arises by records falling into the wrong hands or being misused. The FTC only argues that that data 'could' have been discovered by people online.

The FTC also appears to some to be arguing that the mere fact of a breach represents negligent data security practices, no matter what those practices actually were. (This is potentially troublesome because even the most comprehensive, responsible cybersecurity protocols can never guarantee total immunity from data breaches.)

For his part, Michael Daugherty continues to argue that the overview of LabMD should have been handled exclusively by the Office for Civil Rights (OCR) at the Department of Health and Human Services, as part of their authority to regulate HIPAA compliance.

"If I lose, every healthcare facility in the country loses. They're going to push that they've got jurisdiction to come after healthcare facilities without standards, without notice and over and above Health and Human Services. That's terrifying."

*The trend towards throwing new laws at everything
continues apace.*

John Gardner

Chapter 6. Data Security Laws

I f the direct costs and reputational damage from a data security breach weren't bad enough on their own, small and medium-sized businesses now also face the prospect of having to deal with data security regulations and potential liability, along with the possibility of required future audits for years (and even decades) into the future.

It's important to note that in this regulatory environment, not only are government agencies increasing audits and compliance activities, but employees, vendors, customers and even competitors can report security vulnerabilities or bad practices and several government agencies post violators on public websites, in press releases and even report violations to local media to inform potentially harmed consumers.

In this chapter, we'll take a look at the major laws and agencies that regulate IT security for small businesses.

HIPAA

For medical practices in regards to data security, the law that mandates the most compliance requirements is the Health Insurance Portability and Accounting Act (HIPAA), which President Clinton signed into law in 1996. For our purposes, HIPAA governs ePHI, or electronic protected health information. All medical practices must safeguard this electronic patient medical data, both through proper technologies and proper personnel practices. Unauthorized disclosure of electronic medical data can result in penalties from the Department of Health and Human Services' Office of Civil Rights (OCR). Since the passage of the HITECH Act in 2009, which updated HIPAA rules regarding electronic data, OCR has stepped up their audits of medical practices of all sizes. The FTC has also claimed jurisdiction over data breaches for all types of businesses, including medical practices.

OCR lists four standards regarding types of data breaches and their penalties for medical practices and businesses handling protected patient data.

The first level is for an individual that did not know (and by existing reasonable diligence would not have known) that he/she violated

HIPAA. The minimum penalty is $100 per violation with an annual maximum of $25,000 for repeated violations and the maximum penalty is $50,000.00 per violation with an annual maximum of $1.5 million.

The second level is for a HIPAA violation due to reasonable cause and not due to willful neglect. The minimum penalty is $1,000 per violation with an annual maximum of $100,000.00 for repeat violations and the maximum penalty is $50,000.00 per violation with an annual maximum of $1.5 million.

The third level is a HIPAA violation due to willful neglect but the violation is corrected within the required time period. The minimum penalty is $10,000.00 per violation, with an annual maximum of $250,000.00 for repeat violations and the maximum is $50,000.00 per violation with an annual maximum of $1.5 million.

The fourth and final level is a HIPAA violation that is due to willful neglect and is not corrected. There is one penalty standard for this level, which is $50,000.00 per violation, with an annual maximum of $1.5 million for repeated violations.

PCI

The Payment Card Industry Data Security Standard (PCI DSS) is a proprietary information security standard developed by the Payment Card Industry Security Standards Council, a collaboration among the major credit card brands to decrease fraud and identity theft. It covers organizations that handle transactions involving Visa, MasterCard, American Express, Discover and JCB. It is administered by the Payment Card Industry Security Standards Council. Businesses that are covered by PCI are required to submit validation of compliance annually.

The PCI standards include 12 requirements organized into six 'control objectives.' The six control objectives are:

1. Build and maintain a secure network.
2. Protect cardholder data.
3. Maintain a vulnerability management program.
4. Implement strong access control measures.
5. Regularly monitor and test networks.
6. Maintain an information security policy.

The 12 specific requirements (in order of the objectives with which they are associated) are:

1. Install and maintain a firewall configuration to protect cardholder data.
2. Do not use vendor-supplied defaults for system passwords and other security parameters.
3. Protect stored cardholder data.
4. Encrypt transmission of cardholder data across open, public networks.

5. Use and regularly update anti-virus software on all systems commonly affected by malware.
6. Develop and maintain secure systems and applications.
7. Restrict access to cardholder data by business to need-to-know.
8. Assign a unique ID to each person with computer access.
9. Restrict physical access to cardholder data.
10. Track and monitor all access to network resources and cardholder data.
11. Regularly test security systems and processes
12. Maintain a policy that addresses information security

The penalties for PCI violations can be extensive. They include:

A. Fines up to $500,000.00 per data security incident.
B. Fines up to $50,000.00 per day for non-compliance with published standards.
C. Paying for the cost of re-issuing cards due to the breach.
D. Suspension of the business' merchant account.

PCI compliance does not look broadly across an entire business' network. Rather, it's focused on the databases that store credit card information. This includes things like SSL and

TLS certificates for websites and making sure that any vendors offering web-based solutions can provide attestation of their own PCI compliance. PCI is an evolving standard that is updated regularly.

It is worth noting that all businesses appear to be coming under cybersecurity regulation as the FTC is interpreting companies that are lax with data security and allow breaches to be engaged in 'unfair' and 'deceptive' business practices. While the FTC does not have an official set of regulations regarding cybersecurity, their standards of what constitutes bad practices can be deduced from the settlement statements they issue about companies that they have sanctioned for bad practices.

Further, many individual states have cybersecurity and electronic data protection laws on their books and States Attorney Generals are increasingly showing a willingness to enforce these against companies that allow breaches through bad practices.

Steps To Take

In general, the practices that are outlined in this book in other chapters are ones that will allow your business to be digitally secure and move a great deal toward being compliant. However, each set of regulations has its own specific requirements. It makes most sense for a business to work with an IT company that has a specific protocol for ensuring that your business takes all of the necessary, specific steps to be in compliance, reduce liability and allow your business to withstand an audit.

*For an unarmed man may be attacked with
greater confidence than an armed man.*

Thomas Jefferson

Chapter 7. Network and Workstation Security

In 2016, cybercrime is a major concern for all businesses, especially those with under 200 employees. Making sure networks and computers are secure takes planning and prioritization, but it should not be seen as—and need not be—an overwhelming endeavor.   Let's look at some of the key steps these businesses should be taking to secure themselves from cybercriminals.

Up-To-Date Operating Systems

One of the major, most common cybersecurity vulnerabilities small businesses face is using outdated operating systems—in particular, outdated versions of Windows. The reason this vulnerability is so prevalent is because it's so easy to understand how it arises—that old version of Windows XP is getting the job done on a day-to-day basis, so why invest the money in upgrading? Security is the single best reason for any business to have the latest operating system. Each release of an operating system is designed (mostly) with an eye toward improving security against known threats. And current operating systems are supported by their makers (again, we're normally talking about Microsoft here) with security updates as new vulnerabilities become known. Hackers know vulnerabilities in old operating systems and they will seek out systems using old operating systems. Why make your business an active target?

You may need to upgrade some of your line-of-business applications to work with the latest operating system, but it is well worth the investment. And these operating systems typically deliver enhanced and expanded productivity tools. In particular, with cloud-based (or SAAS—Software-As-A-Service) operating systems like Office 365 that operate on a subscription model, you can avoid having to make a more significant up-front capital expenditure to upgrade.

Updated Security Software

The security software (anti-virus and anti-malware) that a business uses also needs to be regularly updated across all endpoints to respond to increasing and newly-developed threats. Almost any managed services offering from an IT support company will include managing these updates, as it's critical to security and network function—and to decreasing the amount of time that IT companies will need to spend in the future resolving issues. For companies in industries that have their data security practices regulated, documentation of maintaining these updates will have to be provided in case of an audit. Simply installing anti-malware and anti-virus software is not enough and does not protect a business on an ongoing basis.

Patched Business Applications

Line-of-business applications should also be regularly updated with security patches. Security patches (or updates) fix specific, identified vulnerabilities in software applications and are distributed by the developers of the software. Again, managing patches for software is something almost all managed services providers will do as part of any package. One of the best practices in updating patches is to work with an IT provider who uses 'whitelisted' patches. These are security patches that have been installed on a number of devices and tested to make sure that they do not themselves cause other unwanted issues.

Secure Network Configuration

The set-up of your network also needs to be secure. In many businesses, a Windows domain is used. This is a type of computer network in which all user accounts are registered with a central server (or group of severs) known as a domain controller. Active Directory is the Microsoft product that allows for centralized user management, allowing administrators to monitor and control user access to various network resources.

The first line of defense for your business network is a firewall. A firewall is like a traffic cop for your network—it's a device that regulates network access from trusted or untrusted areas. Typically, a firewall will be regulating access to a small business network from the internet. Your firewall will regulate traffic to your network based on access controls that you define. Simply installing a firewall is not enough—it should be continually managed. This service is becoming an increasingly standard offering of IT support companies. Firewall management ensures that the firewall is online and operating as it should be and that settings are up to date. It also allows for appropriate and timely responses to any alerts.

Secure Wireless Networks

Wireless networks are very common in small businesses today and can be installed for not very much money. Securing them is an important step in securing your digital data. There are several important steps that should be taken to make a wireless network secure. Make sure that your wireless access point (or router) has a secure password—one that you devise. Do not simply leave the manufacturer default password in place. You should also limit the strength of your wireless network so that, to the extent possible, it is not broadcast beyond your office area. Most wireless access points continually broadcast the SSID because it makes it automatic for new users to find and identify the network. Turn this feature off and make your network less obvious to find for neighbors and random people.

Use WPA encryption on your wireless network, which is harder to hack, instead of WEP encryption (although you should still use WEP if you don't have an alternative). Even better, many newer access points allow for WPA2 encryption, which provides even stronger security. You should use MAC filtering. MAC, or media access control, is a unique number assigned to devices in a network. By using MAC filtering, you can limit which devices are able to access your wireless network. Though MAC filtering can be circumvented by skilled people, it's still a good idea to use.

Email Security

Email is one of the central technology pieces of modern business. There are two main considerations regarding security when it comes to email: encryption and spam. Encrypting emails when sending them can make sense for a lot of businesses, and is a particularly good idea for businesses in regulated industries. Spam can be not only a productivity killer, but today it can also include dangerous phishing emails. Having a spam-filtering solution is an important element of email security.

Data Loss Prevention

Data loss prevention (DLP) is another key element of business data security. Especially for businesses that are in regulated industries, there is a need to make sure that private data is not inadvertently shared. This type of data can be financial data (including credit card numbers), customer data, and intellectual property. Today's DLP solutions allow administrators to set very granular controls that allow or disallow certain types of information to be shared. One neat example is software that will recognize if a credit card number is being included in an email and not allow that to happen. Controls can also be set to dictate who does and does not have access to certain documents and who is able to share those documents.

Compliant Cloud Providers

Finally, with so many businesses today accessing various solutions hosted in the cloud, it's important to make sure that your cloud solutions providers are hosting their solutions in secure, compliant environments. All of the major public cloud providers are doing so, but it's important to check regardless, especially if your software provider for a specific piece of software is a smaller company.

Mobile phones are one of the most insecure devices that were ever available,...

Evgeny Morozov

Chapter 8. Securing Mobile Devices

B YOD (Bring Your Own Device) has become a part of doing business today for many organizations. Allowing employees to use their own personal devices for business purposes is an attractive option for employees who get to use the device they like best and an attractive option for employers, who get to avoid investing in mobile hardware for employees. The challenge, of course, is making sure that the business data being used on those devices remains secure.

Before we take a look at the best steps to take to secure mobile devices, let's take a look at the data security risks that mobile devices present. Some recent data suggests that many employees (and presumably business owners as well) don't really understand the data risk associated with mobile devices. This is dangerous—lost mobile devices that are accessed by criminals is one of the leading means of data theft. Imagine an employee leaving an iPad at Starbucks after a short meeting and all of a sudden a stranger may have unrestricted access to your sales and client database information—valuable data should he or she wish to sell it to a competitor. Or how about the angry former employee who has been let go who still has downloaded company documents with critical intellectual property on his Android? Unsecured mobile devices can lead to HIPAA, PCI and SOX compliance violations, identity theft, data theft, unauthorized access to social media and other public-facing accounts and brand and reputation damage.

Fortunately, there are increasingly good solutions available for mitigating these risks and they are not difficult to implement. The major approach to securing mobile device data comes from the approach adopted by enterprises. It's called Mobile Device Management (MDM). [Mobile Application Management (MAM) is sometimes listed as a totally separate practice, but we'll include it under MDM here. Both MDM and MAM are generally understood to be components of the broader corporate approach to mobile computing in general, Enterprise Mobility Management (EMM).]

MDM refers to the administration of mobile devices through the use of a software tool. Today, the trend is for MDM to be cloud-based and provide a web-accessible management console that can be used either by an in-house IT staff or an outsourced IT partner (or both). MDM gives companies the ability to set usage policies and control data access and sharing.

Remote Wipe

One of the core features of MDM is the ability for a business to remote wipe a mobile device that has been reported lost or stolen. (In fact, many MDM solutions will give administrators a heads-up that something might be amiss prior to an employee reporting a device is lost by indicating via remote monitoring that the device is not being recently used or that it has gone outside defined geographical boundaries.) While some remote wipes are set to erase the entire content of a mobile device, a better option is to have business data and personal data (on an employee's personal device) segregated, with the ability to only wipe business data and applications if needed. All major MDM solutions will allow administrators to return a phone to the state it was prior to enrolling in mobile management, with all documents, folders, passwords, applications and configurations from the business removed. There is also the ability to be more granular with a remote wipe, removing only certain files and folders.

At the outset of an MDM implementation, it's important to let employees know that their personal data will not be accessed by administrators and will not be wiped. It's also important to communicate the critical nature of protecting business data on mobile devices. Both of these ideas will encourage employees to more quickly report lost or stolen devices.

Securing Access

Mobile devices should be set to require a PIN to access them after they've been left unattended for a short period. MDM solutions can allow for this setting to be implemented on employees' mobile devices, even when they were not set-up to do so previously.

Applications Management

MDM solutions can allow businesses to set determinations about what business applications can be run on a mobile device and how they can be accessed and used. One of the restrictions that can be set-up, for example, is to only allow employees to edit Office documents securely in the business versions of the Office suite accessed on the phone, and not insecurely on personal versions of Office software that may also be installed on the phone. This type of control can be applied to emails and their software, limiting the ability to download attachments onto the personal space of a mobile device and also limiting the ability to cut and past data from secure business emails.

When you fall, get right back up.

Lindsey Vonn

Chapter 9. Data Back-Up

Having a data back-up and disaster recovery solution for your business is critical. Today, it really is like an essential form of business insurance. What would the cost be in liability, lost productivity and simply lost records if you were to get caught without one?

Perhaps your response is that the likelihood of a disaster striking your practice is low. Well, that depends on what we're thinking of when we talk about disasters. Disasters that disrupt networks and destroy electronic records usually aren't hurricanes, tornadoes or floods. They're much more likely to be mundane accidents like coffee spilled on a computer or a small fire from a connection overheating in the server closet or a sprinkler system errantly turning on or an employee error. Network disasters are much more common than natural disasters. In general, the world of business owners who are considering back-up and disaster recovery can be divided into those who have experienced a data loss and those who haven't. Don't wait to be in the former category to take care of this essential planning.

Cloud-Based Back-Up

So let's talk about what you should be considering when implementing a back-up and disaster recovery solution. First, you want to be backing up your data and network in the cloud. You may use a hybrid solution, which backs up your data on both an on-premise hard drive and the cloud, but the cloud should definitely be a part of your solution. Why? Because the cloud actually affords you more security than on-premise or local solutions. I know that for many business owners, this seems odd. Keeping the data on-site, close-by intuitively seems to be the more secure solution. But consider where your data is residing when it's in 'the cloud'. It is actually going to the highly secure, redundant data centers of major technology vendors.

These data centers are designed to secure electronic data—from the technology used to the physical design of the building to the personnel.

The data that resides in them is encrypted and it is also encrypted in transit to these data centers. These centers meet HIPAA and other safety standards. In short, they provide more secure situations for data than residing in a medical practice.

RTO, RPO and Fail-Over

Current cloud back-up solutions do not simply copy your data either. They are managed software solutions that have web-based portals that allow for testing and monitoring and provide alerts if there are issues with backing-up the data. These solutions are often monitored by the practice's outsourced IT partner.

Modern data back-up solutions also allow you to control how frequently your data is backed up (for example, every 24 hours, every six hours, every 15 minutes...) and how quickly you can recover that data.

These two measures are known as Recovery Point Objective (RPO) and Recovery Time Objective (RTO), respectively. Cloud based data back-up solutions can also allow your team to keep working through a network disaster, by replicating your network in the cloud and providing fail-over operability there. So long as internet access is still available, all workstations, software and processes can be accessed in the cloud in real time.

Personnel Practices

Outside of the technology safeguards that need to be implemented to back-up your data in case of a disaster, there should also be appropriate staff procedures in place for such an event. Does everybody on staff know what to do in case of a disaster? Do they know how to use the technology appropriately in such a situation and what the technology back-up solution is? These are important considerations that should be part of regular planning and training.

Having a reliable managed data back-up system is perhaps the most critical component of securing your business against cyberattack today. It ensures that in the case of a successful attack, you will be able to access the data you need. It provides an essential peace-of-mind to business owners. And it's also important to note that it can provide an important peace-of-mind to customers. Many more customers today are obviously aware of the dangers to data posed by cybercriminals and cyberattacks, and having the ability to promote the data security integrity best-practices of your business can be a marketing differentiator.

   With today's ransomware attacks generating so many situations in which victimized businesses cannot access their primary source of data, not having a back-up you know you can trust is just not a risk worth taking.

To err is human....

Alexander Pope

Chapter 10. Employee Training and Policies

In today's technology environment, it may seem ironic that the last line of defense against cybercriminals is humans. In fact, employee training can make a very big difference in helping your business avoid attack. At the outset, it's important to simply communicate to your employees the value of the data your business handles, the liability the company can face if it's mishandled and the pain it can cause for customers if their data is revealed.

Here are some sensible steps every business can take to help their employees better protect company data.

Create strong passwords. Leaving default passwords or having weak, obvious passwords is not acceptable. Programs should also be in place to ensure that employees need to update their passwords every few months. Additionally, two-factor verification is a very good practice to follow.

Ensure that employees have the "lowest-level required access" to do their jobs. Not every employee needs access to every part of the business' network, and allowing employees to enter parts of the network where they have no business to conduct simply expands the potential for damaging behavior. When employees do stop working at the business, make sure that your IT provider is notified promptly and their accounts and access are removed. The same holds true when work stops for contractors that were given access to the network.

How do your employees handle certain types of email, like requests from superiors to send money to a third party, or requests from vendors for information? Is there a verification process set-up? Hackers have been known to access company data and send 'internal' emails disguised to be from senior executives ordering fraudulent payments to be made.   Make sure your team has a process in place, like calling a senior executive or a contact at a vendor to ensure legitimacy.

Make sure your employees are aware of the prevalence and danger of phishing today. Make sure they can identify some of the more common tell-tale signs of phishing emails and that they know never to click on a link in an unsolicited email. Also make sure that employees never click on strange pop-up boxes, even to click the 'x' in the top corner to close them. They should simply hit Alt-F4 to close the window.

Finally, make sure employees are aware of the threat posed by mobile devices and mobile media solutions like USB drives falling into the wrong hands. Workplaces get busy, but simply reminding employees of the threat posed by treating these devices casually can make a big difference. The real cost of the loss of one of these devices is not the money to replace the hardware—it's the potential liability and repercussions from lost data.

Incomprehensible jargon is the hallmark of a profession.

Kingman Brewster, Jr.

Glossary

Active Directory

The Microsoft product that allows for centralized user management, allowing administrators to monitor and control user access to various network resources.

Advanced Persistent Threats

A sophisticated network attack in which a hacker gains access to a network and stays there undetected for an extended period, usually with the intent of stealing data.

Bitcoin

A digital payment system that is difficult to trace and is commonly used to collect ransomware ransom payments.

Botnets

A network of computers owned by various people that has been secretly infected with malicious software and is controlled to perform illegal activities.

BYOD

Bring-Your-Own-Device is the practice of allowing employees to use their own mobile devices for business activities.

Data Loss Prevention

An approach for ensuring employees don't share protected data with unauthorized outsiders.

Denial of Service Attacks

DoS attacks are designed to make computers or networks unavailable, typically by overloading them with traffic.

Firewall

Software or hardware designed to regulate traffic in and out of computer networks.

FTC

The Federal Trade Commission is the government agency increasingly asserting authority to regulate commercial cybersecurity practices.

HIPAA

The Health Insurance Portability and Accountability Act defines acceptable practices for healthcare businesses to secure patient data.

The Internet Crime Complaint Center

Also known as IC3, the place to report suspected cybercrimes to the federal government.

Lowest-Level Required Access

The practice of limiting individual employee access to only needed parts of a business network.

MAC Filtering

The practice of limiting network access based on the MAC addresses of computers.

Malvertising

The use of online advertising to spread malware.

Malware

A variety of malicious software designed to infect and do harm to computers and networks.

MDM

Mobile Device Management is the administration of mobile devices through a software platform.

OCR

The Office of Civil Rights at the Department of Health and Human Services, which has enforcement responsibilities for HIPAA digital security requirements.

Patching

For security purposes, the process of updating software to remove vulnerabilities.

PCI-DSS

The proprietary standard for digital security covering businesses that accept credit cards.

Phishing Emails

Emails from cybercriminals designed to look like emails from legitimate sources, which are used to collect information or access.

Ransomware

A type of malware designed to block access to a network or data until a ransom is paid.

Remote Monitoring

The practice of having an IT company or staff maintain monitoring of computers or networks through the use of embedded software and internet connections.

Remote Wipe

The process of removing business data and applications from an employee's mobile device when it is lost or stolen.

RPO

The Recovery Point Objective is the maximum amount of time that data can be left without back-up in a managed back-up implementation.

RTO

The Recovery Time Objective is the amount of time after a disaster targeted for having business processes restored in a managed back-up implementation.

Social Engineering

The practice of cybercriminals preying on human vulnerabilities of employees to trick them into granting access or information.

Two-Factor Authentication

Also known as 2FA, is a security practice requiring an additional piece of private information beyond a password to grant access.

Virus

Malicious software code that has the ability to copy itself.

WPA2

An encryption standard for wireless networks that is stronger that the alternatives of WPA and WEP.

Zero-Day Vulnerability

A software vulnerability that is unknown to the developer of the software and can be exploited by cybercriminals.

.

www.ingramcontent.com/pod-product-compliance
Lightning Source LLC
Chambersburg PA
CBHW022111170526
45157CB00004B/1584